W9-CFB-312

CH

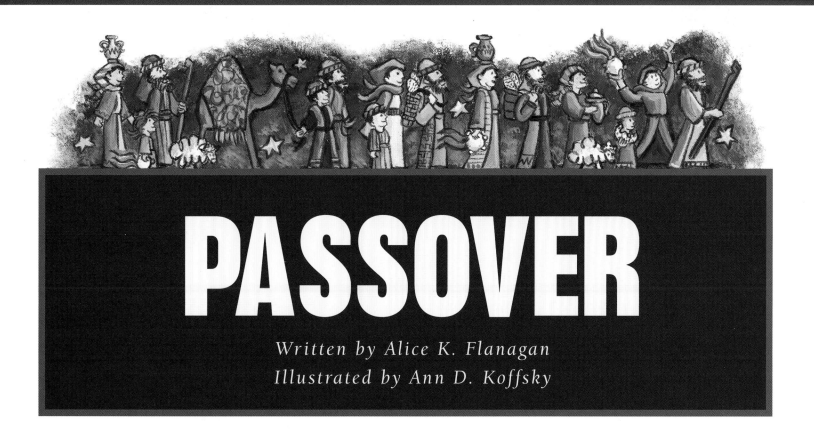

PASSOVER

Written by Alice K. Flanagan
Illustrated by Ann D. Koffsky

Content Adviser: Ina S. G. Regosin, Dean of Students, Hebrew College, Newton, Massachusetts

Reading Adviser: Dr. Linda D. Labbo, Department of Reading Education, College of Education, The University of Georgia

C O M P A S S   P O I N T   B O O K S

M I N N E A P O L I S ,   M I N N E S O T A

Compass Point Books
3109 West 50th Street, #115
Minneapolis, MN 55410

Visit Compass Point Books on the Internet at *www.compasspointbooks.com*
or e-mail your request to *custserv@compasspointbooks.com*

Editors: E. Russell Primm, Emily J. Dolbear, and Patricia Stockland
Designer: The Design Lab

Library of Congress Cataloging-in-Publication Data
Flanagan, Alice K.
 Passover / written by Alice K. Flanagan ; illustrated by Ann Koffsky.
    p. cm. — (Holidays and festivals)
Includes bibliographical references and index.
 ISBN 0-7565-0481-3 (hc : alk. paper)
 1. Passover—Juvenile literature. 2. Seder—Juvenile literature. I. Koffsky, Ann D. II. Title.
III. Holidays and festivals (Compass Point Books)
BM695.P3F64 2003
296.4'37—dc21   2002155736

Table of Contents

NOTE: In this book, words that are defined in the glossary are in **bold** *the first time they appear in the text.*

Once we were slaves. God set us free. God led us through the desert to a land of plenty.

These are words you might hear spoken during Passover. It is a holiday **celebrated** by Jews all over the world during the spring season. The Hebrew name for Passover is *Pesach*.

Passover is a celebration of freedom! It is a time when Jews remember how God "passed over" their homes and saved them from the **plagues**. They also remember how their ancestors "passed over" from slavery to freedom. Many people believe the Passover story is one of the most important events in the life of the Jewish people. For some Jews, the Passover celebration lasts eight days.

In the Land of Egypt

About four thousand years ago, the Jewish people left their homeland and went to Egypt in search of food. Egypt is a country in northern Africa. The Jews were happy there until **Pharaoh**, the king of Egypt, made them slaves. For many years, Pharaoh forced the Jews to build cities for him. He worked them hard and treated them badly.

The Jews prayed to God to free them from their unhappy lives. According to legend, God heard their prayers and sent a simple **shepherd** named Moses to them. God told Moses to take the Jews back to their homeland, where they would be safe and free. For more than a year, Moses asked Pharaoh to free the Jews. Again and again, Pharaoh said no. Each time Pharaoh refused, terrible plagues covered the land.

People died of strange illnesses. Wind and hail knocked down houses. Frogs and insects destroyed crops. When Pharaoh's own son died, the king finally ordered Moses to take the Jews and go.

The Trip to the Promised Land

Moses and the Jews left Egypt in a hurry. They did not have time to prepare for the journey. They took only what they could carry. People quickly made bread to take with them. They made it flat because there was no time to put yeast in it and wait for it to rise. They called the flat bread *matzah* (MOT-za).

In the desert, God showed Moses the way to go. During the day, God became a cloud that Moses followed. At night, God was a pillar of fire to light the way.

Soon after the Jews had left Egypt, Pharaoh changed his mind about letting them go free. He sent out soldiers to bring them back. The soldiers found the Jews by the Red Sea as they were trying to cross it. God helped the Jews. He told Moses to raise his arm over the sea. Just then the waters rolled back so the Jews could cross to the other side.

The soldiers followed, but the sea came crashing down on them. They all drowned. The Jews were safe at last. They began their journey to **Canaan**, the land that God had promised to them. Many years later, the Jews arrived in Canaan, which is now the state of Israel. The people immediately held a feast.

How Did
Passover Begin?

Forty years after Moses led the Jews out of Egypt, they arrived in Canaan and held a feast to celebrate their freedom. They thanked God for the kindness He had shown to them and talked about what He had done for them. They remembered the trip their grandparents had taken from Egypt. Then they shared a meal of roasted lamb, matzah, and green vegetables, just as their grandparents had done.

As the years passed, one of the villages in Canaan became a large city called **Jerusalem.** The Jews built a great Temple there to pray in. Soon, Jews from all over the land came to celebrate Passover in the Temple. They added music and singing to the celebration.

Over time, the Passover holiday changed. Soon, Jews were living in many lands. Some of them had forgotten how to celebrate Passover. Jewish leaders called **rabbis** wrote down a set of rules for Passover that everyone could follow.

How Is Passover Celebrated Today?

Today, most Jews celebrate Passover in much the same way as the early Jews did. To prepare for the holiday, they clean their homes. Then they put out the special dishes that will be used for the Passover meal. All bread except matzah is removed from the house. Some Jews stop working on the first two days and last two days of Passover.

The holiday begins with a service called a *Seder* (SAY-der). Seder means "order of service." The Seder is held on either the first night or the first two nights of Passover. During the Seder, Jews eat special foods to remind them of how hard life was in the desert for their ancestors. They are each given a *Haggadah* (hah-GAH-dah), which is a book about the Passover story. Haggadah means "to tell." Jews read aloud from the Haggadah.

The Seder Meal

Before the Seder begins, candles are lit and the table is set. People wash their hands. Then a prayer or blessing is said over the wine or grape juice that everyone will drink. The wine or grape juice stands for joy. During the Seder, each person drinks four cups of wine or grape juice.

A special cloth or tray is placed on the table with three pieces of matzah. A piece from the middle matzah is broken off and hidden somewhere in the house. This piece is called the *afikomen* (afi-KOH-men). At the end of the Seder, children look for the afikomen. The child who finds it wins a special gift. Then the afikomen is broken into many parts and shared with everyone.

During the Seder, families and guests sit at the table. They eat special foods. Before the meal begins, they eat matzah to remind them of the flat bread the Jews ate when they left Egypt. Then they eat the special food from the Seder plate.

Why Tell the Passover Story?

During the Seder meal, the Haggadah, or Passover story, is read. It is read every year to remind Jews of their past and to teach children the history of their people. Usually, the youngest child at the Seder begins the story by asking and answering four questions.

1. Why is this night different from all other nights?
On this night we eat only matzah. On other nights, we eat matzah and bread.

2. On all other nights we eat all kinds of vegetables. Why do we eat only bitter vegetables on this night?
These vegetables remind us of the bitterness of slavery.

Peace and Freedom for the World

As the Seder comes to a close, children look for the hidden afikomen. It is the last food everyone eats at the Seder. Afterward, everyone gives thanks for the food they have eaten and the life they share as free people. They wish for peace throughout the world and sing songs of joy. Everyone drinks a final cup of wine or grape juice and talks about celebrating Passover again next year. They say, "Maybe next year we will all meet in Jerusalem!"

Things You Might See During Passover

Matzah

Matzah is bread that does not rise because it contains no yeast. The flat, dry bread is eaten throughout the weeklong Passover holiday. Matzah is made of flour and water. Holes are punched in the dough to keep it from rising. It is baked no more than eighteen minutes. Eating matzah gives Jews a taste of slavery and an appreciation for freedom.

The Seder Plate

In the center of every Seder table is a Seder plate with five foods on it. There are bitter herbs called *maror* (ma-ROAR). Horseradish is an example of maror. People eat maror to remind them of how bitter slavery is. A green vegetable such as parsley, lettuce, or celery, is also on the plate. It is called *karpas* (CAR-pas) and is a reminder of spring. Before eating karpas, people dip it into saltwater to remind them of the bitter tears the Jews cried when they were slaves. *Haroset* (har-OH-set) is on the plate, too. It is a mixture made from chopped apples, nuts, cinnamon, and wine. Haroset looks like the mortar Jewish slaves used to make brick buildings in Egypt. The last two foods on the plate are a boiled egg and a roasted lamb or chicken leg bone. The bone reminds people of the lamb the Jews offered up to God during their first Passover celebration. The boiled egg is a sign of new life.

The Haggadah

Haggadah is a Hebrew word that means "to tell." The Haggadah is a guidebook for Jewish families. It tells them what to do and when and how to do it during the many parts of the Passover ceremony. Families also read the Passover story from the Haggadah. The Haggadah is very old, but new ideas have been added to it over the years. Today, you can buy a modern Haggadah to get ideas for Passover plays and Seder activities.

What You Can Do During Passover

Passover is a Jewish holiday. It celebrates Jewish freedom. Passover has meaning for all people who love freedom, however. Here are some things you can do during Passover.

* Share something you have with someone who has less than you.
* Think of ways you can help make the world a better place.
* Make up your own blessing for your family, friends, and the world.
* Write down questions you would like to ask about the Passover story.
* Write a play about freedom.
* Help your parents, grandparents, or friends prepare a Seder meal. Make a place card for each guest. Then decorate the cards with pictures of the Passover story.

Glossary

ancestors a person's grandparents, great-grandparents, and so on

Canaan a region between the country of Jordan and the Mediterranean Sea

celebrated had a party or honored a special event

Jerusalem the capital of Israel

mortar a mixture that is used to lay bricks in a building

Pharaoh the title of the rulers of ancient Egypt

plagues things that cause great suffering or trouble

rabbis teachers of Jewish law who are usually leaders of a congregation

shepherd a person who takes care of sheep

Where You Can Learn More about Passover

At the Library

Bat-Ami, Miriam. *Dear Elijah*. Philadelphia: Jewish Publication Society, 1997.

Hoyt-Goldsmith, Diane, and Lawrence Migdale. *Celebrating Passover*. New York: Holiday House, 2000.

Simon, Norma, and Erika Weihs. *The Story of Passover*. New York: HarperTrophy, 1998.

Zwebner, Janet. *Uh! Oh! Passover Haggadah*. New York: Pitspopany Press, 2002.

On the Web

Kids Domain: Holidays
http://www.kidsdomain.com/holiday/passover/
For information and links about Passover

Passover.net
http://www.passover.net/scripts/tgij/paper/passoverTemplate.asp?ArticleID=1981
For Passover games and stories

Through the Mail

The Magnes Museum
Administrative Offices
166 Geary, Suite 1500
San Francisco, CA 94108
For information on Jewish history, culture, and art throughout the world

On the Road

The Jewish Museum
1109 Fifth Avenue at 92nd Street
New York, NY 10128
212/423-3200
To view art and history exhibits about Jewish culture

National Museum of American Jewish History
55 North 5th Street
Philadelphia, PA 19106
215/923-3811
To view over 10,000 artifacts related to American Jewish history and culture

Index

About the Author and Illustrator

Alice K. Flanagan writes books for children and teachers. Since she was a young girl, she has enjoyed writing. She has written more than seventy books. Some of her books include biographies of U.S. presidents and their wives, biographies of people working in our neighborhoods, phonics books for beginning readers, and informational books about birds and Native Americans. Alice K. Flanagan lives in Chicago, Illinois.

Ann D. Koffsky has illustrated more than ten books for children. She created the illustrations in this book with acrylic paints and colored pencils on bristol paper. Passover in the Koffsky house is always a cheerful family gathering, and Ann is looking forward to using a copy of this book at her next Seder meal. Ann lives in West Hempstead, New York, with her husband Mark, and their two children, Aaron and Jeremy.

j296.437 Flanagan, Alice K.
FLA
        Passover.

$22.60

DATE			